FOR YOUNG VOICES

SOMETHING NEW TO SING ABOUT

CHORAL LITERATURE for 2 PART SSA MALE ENSEMBLES

Glencoe

G. SCHIRMER, Inc.

CONTENTS

4

An American Salute

America - When Johnny Comes Marching Home Again
Shenandoah - Battle Hymn Of The Republic

Performance Notes:
 Tempo markings are a suggestion only. The director should feel free to perform certain sections of this arrangement a bit slower or faster than indicated. Keep a distinctly different interpretation between verse one of "Johnny Comes Marching" (letter A in minor) and verse two (Letter B in major). This arrangement is particularly well suited for closing any program and can be performed by any size choral ensemble.   E.L.

Arranged by
ED LOJESKI

Traditional

Performance Time: approx. 3:50

Andante (♩ = 88 a bit rubato)

Soprano

My coun-try 'tis of thee, ___

Alto

Electric Guitar

(Guitar tacet until letter [C])   Play

Piano

(for rehearsal only)

Electric Bass

Percussion   S.D. (Sticks)   (S.D.)
                  B.D.

sweet land of lib-er-ty, ___

(Cym.)

A tempo   dim.

of thee I sing. ___

                        Of thee I

(Field Drum)   dim.

AN AMERICAN SALUTE - Two Part

For Amanda
Baloo, Baloo

Words by Richard Gall

Traditional Scottish melody
Arranged by Robert Rhein

* Pronounced "ē"

wee, wee — thing, For thou art dou - bly dear to me.

loo, my wee, wee — thing, For thou art dear to me. But

Thy dad - die's ab - sence long, my wea - ry heart in two,

o, might break, Wert

not left a dar - lin' pledge, the ee - rie hours — a- way.

thou, To steal, Ba -

pp

pp

Be Kind To Your Parents
From the Musical Comedy "FANNY"
Arranged by WILLIAM STICKLES

Words and Music by
HAROLD ROME

18

Be Kind to Your Parents - SA

life. They're apt to be ner-vous, and o-ver ex-

life. They're apt to be ner-vous, and o-ver ex-

cit - ed, Con - fused from their dai - ly storm and

cit - ed, Con - fused from their dai - ly storm and

strife. Just keep in mind,_____ Tho' it sounds

strife. Just keep in mind,_____ Tho' it sounds

Be Kind to Your Parents - SA

odd, I know, ___ Most par - ents once were chil - dren long a-

odd, I know, ___ Most par - ents once were chil - dren long a-

(Spoken)

go. In - cre-di - ble! So treat them with

go. So treat them with

pa - tience and sweet un - der - stand - ing, In

pa - tience and sweet un - der - stand - ing, In

Be Kind to Your Parents - SA

Be Kind to Your Parents - SA

Brother Will, Brother John

Elizabeth Charles Welborn

John Sacco

ain't no use, Mis-ter, af-ter you're gone, ___ You can't take it with you, Broth-er

ain't no use, Mis-ter, af-ter you're gone, ___ You can't take it with you, Broth-er

Will, Broth-er John. You need-n't squeeze your coin tight in your hand, No

Will, Broth-er John. You need-n't squeeze your coin tight in your hand, No

place for small change in the Prom - ised Land. It ain't no use, Mis-ter,

place for small change in the Prom - ised Land. It ain't no use, Mis-ter,

Will, Brother John, Brother Will, Brother John, Brother Will, Broth-er

Will, Brother John, Brother Will, Brother John, Brother Will, Broth-er

John. Why mope a - round with fu -

John. Why mope a - round with fu -

ne - re - al fa - ces, Whip up your nag and loos - en the tra - ces.

ne - re - al fa - ces, Whip up your nag and loos - en the tra - ces.

Free To Be . . . You And Me

(from: Free to Be . . . You and Me)

Bruce Hart

Stephen Lawrence
Arranged by Margaret Vance

32

You and   me,_____   you and   me,

You and   me,_____   you and   me,

You and   me,_____   you and   me,

you and   me._____

you   and   me.

you   and   me._____

The Gypsy Rover

Irish Ballad
Arranged by Margaret Vance

The gyp - sy rov - er came o - ver the hill, And
She left her fa - ther's __ cas - tle gate; She

down thro' the val - ley so shad - y. He whis - tled and he sang __ till the
left her own true __ lov - er; She left her serv - ants and __

green woods rang And he won the heart of a la - dy.
her es - tate To __ fol - low the gyp - sy __ rov - er.

38

whist - ling gyp - sy ___ rov er.

rov - er.

Slightly slower, somewhat freely
[Solo, or a few voices]

"He's no gyp - sy, my fa - ther," said she, "He's

molto rit.

Slightly slower, somewhat freely

lord of free - lands all o - ver; And I will stay till my

And I will stay till my

Hitch Your Dream To The Morning Star

By EUGENE BUTLER

* Available For:
Three Part Mixed, Two Part

44

lift your eyes to the morn- ing sky.

lift your eyes to the morn- ing sky.

17 Warm

Set your goal t'ward the ris- ing sun,—

(Set your goal t'ward the ris- ing sun,—)

17

(with a dream a job can be done.) You can make a dream re-

with a dream a job can be done. You can make re-

HITCH YOUR DREAM TO THE MORNING STAR - Two Part

HITCH YOUR DREAM TO THE MORNING STAR - Two-Part

HITCH YOUR DREAM TO THE MORNING STAR - Two-Part

(melody)

reach the high-est in all you do;— this is my wish,

reach the high-est in all you do;— this is my

this is my wish, my wish _____ for

wish, my wish _____ for

you, _____ for you. _____

you, _____ for you. _____

HITCH YOUR DREAM TO THE MORNING STAR - Two-Part

Hush, My Babe

*James Neal Koudelka
Arranged by Boyd Bacon

Copyright © 1980 G. Schirmer, Inc.
All Rights Reserved   International Copyright Secured   Printed in U. S. A.

Hush my babe, no need for weep - ing, Close your eyes, please do not

Hush my babe, no need for weep - ing, Close your eyes, please do not

cry. You are safe in moth - er's keep - ing,

(melody)

cry. _____ You are safe in moth - er's keep - ing,

Sleep, and heed this lul - la - by. _____

Sleep, and heed this lul - la - by. _____

Soon, my babe, you'll grow and

Soon, my babe, you'll grow and

leave me, Seek your for-tune on your own.

leave me, Seek your for-tune on your own.

Though the thought does of-ten grieve me   This a moth-er's al-ways

(melody)

Though the thought does of-ten grieve me   This a moth-er's al-ways

cresc.

(melody)

known._____   But for now, sleep tight my ba - by, don't cry_____

cresc.

known._____   But for now, sleep tight my ba - by, don't cry__

cresc.

now._____

now._____

mp

molto rit.

I Will Extol Thee, My God

Psalm 145:1, 3, 9

Georg Friedrich Handel
Arranged by Robert S. Hines

54

56

Walt Disney's
It's A Small World
Theme from the Disneyland and Walt Disney World Attraction, "It's A Small World"

Vocal Ranges

PART I   PART II

Performance Notes:

This arrangement is designed for use by the beginning choir and can be used with any combination of voices. Either piano or guitar accompaniment or both may be used. Any combination of rhythm instruments may be used depending on what is available in the classroom. The obbligato part may be played on the bells or any C melody instrument.

Arranged by
ED LOJESKI

Performance time: approx. 1:50

Words and Music by
RICHARD M. SHERMAN
and ROBERT B. SHERMAN

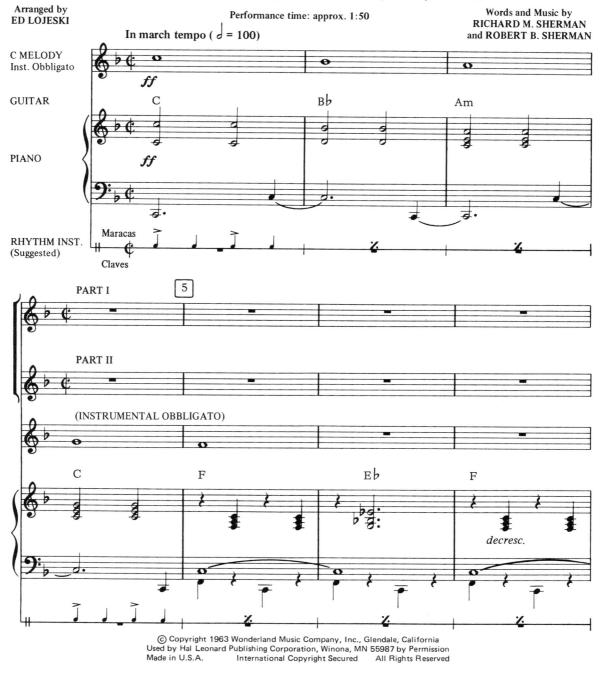

58

It's a world of laugh - ter, a world of

It's a world of laugh - ter, a world of

tears; It's a world of hopes and a world of

tears; It's a world of hopes and a world of

It's A Small World - 2-Part

fears. There's so much that we share that it's

fears. There's so much that we share that it's

F7

time we're a - ware. It's a small world af - ter

time we're a - ware It's a small world af - ter

Bb   Gm7   C7 sus4   C7 sus6   C7

It's A Small World - 2-Part

60

It's A Small World - 2-Part

af - ter all.   It's   a   small   world

af - ter all.   It's   a   small   world

F   F7

To Coda ⊕

af - ter all,   It's a small,   small   world.____

af - ter all,   It's a small,   small   world.____

Bb   Bbm   C7 sus4   C7 sus6 C7   F

It's A Small World - 2-Part

It's A Small World - 2-Part

64

It's A Small World - 2-Part

small world af - ter all.

friend - ship to ev - 'ry one. Though the

It's a small world af - ter

moun - tains di - vide and the o - ceans are

It's A Small World - 2-Part

Mountain Song

Vocal Range:

Words and Music by
CARL J. NYGARD JR.

Performance Time: Approx. 2:30

Moderato (♩ = 96)

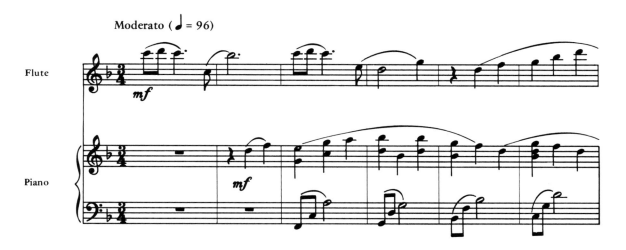

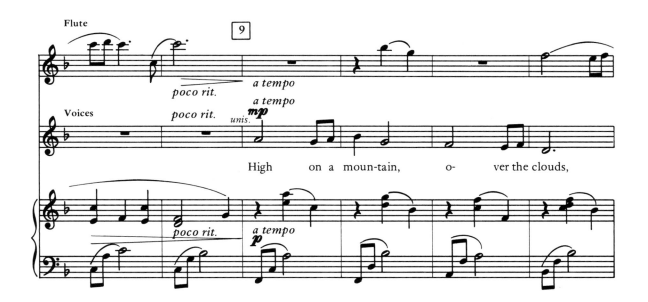

High on a moun-tain, o-ver the clouds,

there where the bald ea- gle flies._____ A song with-out an ech- o was riding the air and it fol-lowed the breeze and start-ed to rise; There might have been more, but I caught it be- fore my mem-o-ry

let its phras- es fall, and I brought back the song, ech-

-o and all._____

MOUNTAIN SONG - 2-Part

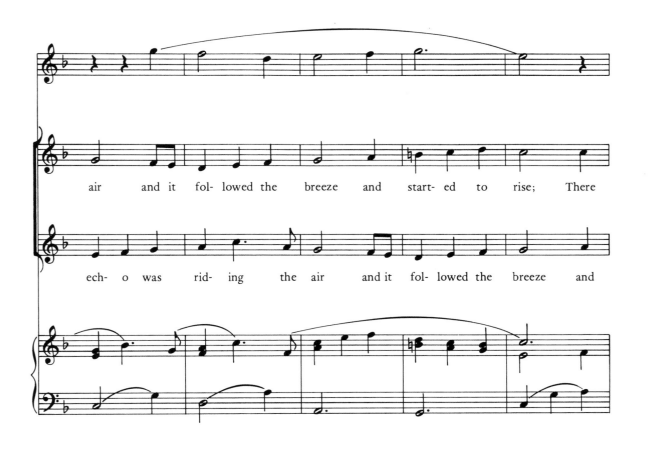

air and it fol- lowed the breeze and start- ed to rise; There

ech- o was rid- ing the air and it fol- lowed the breeze and

might have been more, but I caught it be- fore my mem- o- ry

start- ed to rise; There might have been more, but I caught it be-

Mountain Song

Words and Music by
CARL J. NYGARD JR.

FLUTE

Panis Angelicus
Father Most Merciful

Violoncello

César Franck
Arranged by Carl Deis

Panis Angelicus
Father Most Merciful

This choral arrangement may be used with the original accompaniment of Organ, Harp and 'Cello.

César Franck
Arranged by Carl Deis

Panis Angelicus
Father Most Merciful

Violin
(In place of Violoncello)

César Franck
Arranged by Carl Deis

Prayer
from "Hansel And Gretel"

Stanza 1 translated by **Constance Bache**
(from the German form of the White Paternoster)
Stanza 2 adapted by **Willis Wager**
(from the English forms of the same folk-prayer)

Engelbert Humperdinck
Arranged by Bryceson Treharne

cov - er, Two who o'er me hov - er,
wak - en, May my soul be tak - en,

warm - ly cov - er, Two who o'er me hov - er,
do not wak - en, May my soul be tak - en,

mf
Two to whom 'tis giv - en To guide _____ my
By the Lord be giv - en A home _____ a -

mf
Two to whom 'tis giv - en To guide _____ my
By the Lord be giv - en A home _____ a -

poco rit. *1. a tempo*
steps _____ to heav - en.
bove _____ in

poco rit. *a tempo*
steps _____ to heav - en.
bove _____ in

poco rit. *pp a tempo*

The Shepherds Saw A Star

J. P.

Jean Pasquet

Shep-herds left their flocks ____ and start-ed on their way.

Shep-herds left their flocks and start-ed on their way.

"Can we find the man - ger where the Child is

Slower   a tempo

laid, Son of God, most ho - ly, born ____ of a maid?"

On they pressed though wea - ry, on to Beth-l'hem town. _____

Found the Babe in man - ger, and they bowed them down.

Found the Babe in man - ger, and they bowed them down.

Je - sus, bless - ed Sav - ior, Prince of Peace art

Je - sus, bless ed Sav - ior, Prince of Peace art

S'vivon
(The Dreydl Song)

English text by Alicia Smith

Hanukkah Song
Arranged by Gregg Smith

*It is preferable to sing the first verse in Hebrew and the second in English.

This Train

Arranged By
RUTH ARTMAN

This train is bound for glo - ry, no turn-in' back; We're on the right track; An' a -

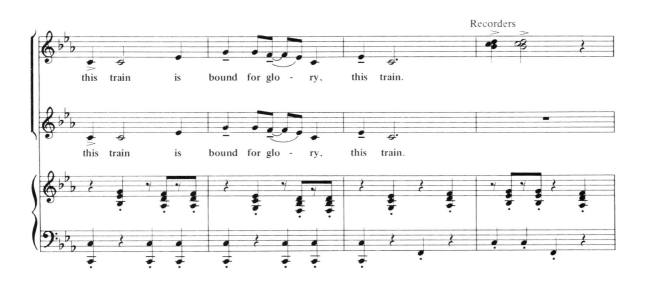

this train is bound for glo - ry, this train.

Recorders

this train is bound for glo - ry, this train.

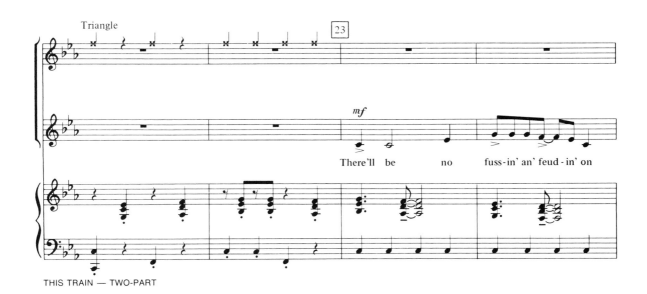

Triangle

23

mf

There'll be no fuss-in' an' feud-in' on

THIS TRAIN — TWO-PART

No - No - No - No!

this train.

There'll be no fuss-in' an' feud - in' on

No - No - No - No!

this train.

There'll be no fuss-in' an' feud - in',

There'll be no fuss-in' an' feud - in', no

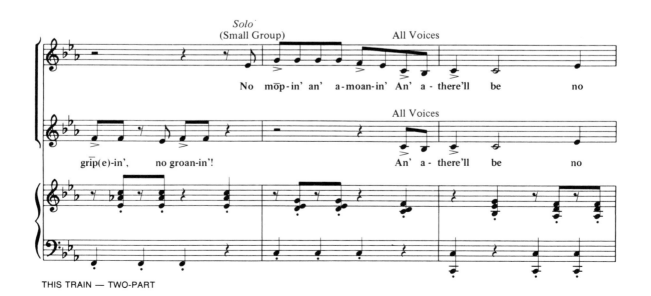

No mōp-in' an' a-moan-in' An' a-there'll be no

grip(e)-in', no groan-in'!

An' a-there'll be no

THIS TRAIN — TWO-PART

THIS TRAIN — TWO-PART

great new won-der-ful day! Whoo-ee-oo!

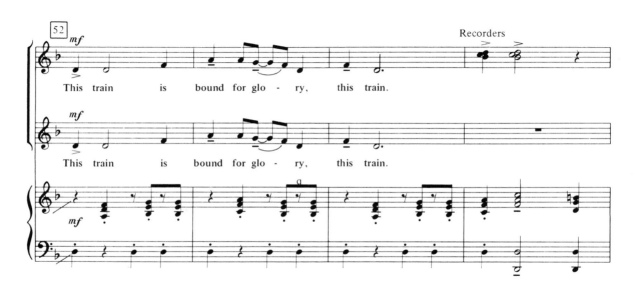

This train is bound for glo-ry, this train.

This train is bound for glo-ry, this train.

This train is bound for glo-ry; this train.

This train is bound for glo-ry; this train.

THIS TRAIN — TWO-PART

This train is bound for glo - ry; no turn-in' back, we're on the right track, An' a -

This train is bound for glo - ry; no turn-in' back, we're on the right track, An' a -

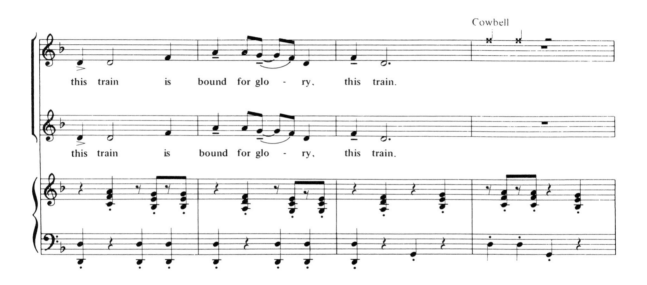

Cowbell

this train is bound for glo - ry, this train.

this train is bound for glo - ry, this train.

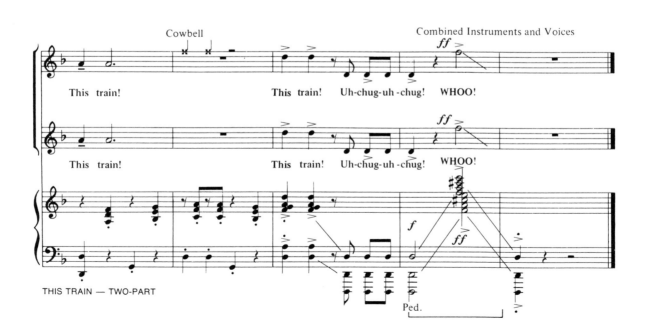

Cowbell

Combined Instruments and Voices

ff

This train!   This train! Uh-chug-uh-chug! WHOO!

This train!   This train! Uh-chug-uh-chug! WHOO!

f

ff

Ped.

THIS TRAIN — TWO-PART

From The WALT DISNEY Motion Picture "PETE'S DRAGON"

Candle On The Water

Performance Notes:
    Keep voices and instruments legato throughout. Work for a very simple (not busy)
feeling. This is not a difficult arrangement and can be learned in a relatively short time.

E.L.

Performance time: approx. 2:55

Arranged by
ED LOJESKI

Words and Music by
AL KASHA and JOEL HIRSCHHORN

Candle On The Water - SSA

100

turn. Ah _____

decresc.

I'll be your can - dle on___ the wa - ter

I'll be your can - dle on___ the wa - ter

(Guitar enter)
C   Dm   F   G   G7

mf (Closed Hi-Hat)

Oo _____

till ev' - ry wave___ is warm and bright. My soul is there be - side you

till ev' - ry wave___ is warm and bright. My soul is there be - side you

C   Am   Bb   G   E7/G#   [15] Am   C7/G

Candle On The Water - SSA

Candle On The Water - SSA

Candle On The Water - SSA

Candle On The Water - SSA

Candle On The Water - SSA

Candle On The Water - SSA

Candle On The Water - SSA

Candle On The Water - SSA

Down Low In The Valley

German Folk Song
English Version by Alice Parker

Collected by Johannes Brahms
Arranged by Ivan Trusler

3. For the time that you loved me, dear, thanks give I

3. For the time that you loved me, dear, thanks give I

3. For the time that you loved me, dear, thanks give I

thee, ___ With the wish that an - o - ther love tru - er may be.

thee, ___ With the wish that an - o - ther love tru - er may be.

thee, With the wish that an - o - ther love tru - er may be.

From Walt Disney's "CINDERELLA"
A Dream Is A Wish Your Heart Makes

Arranged by
DICK AVERRE

Words and Music by
**MACK DAVID, AL HOFFMAN,
JERRY LIVINGSTON**

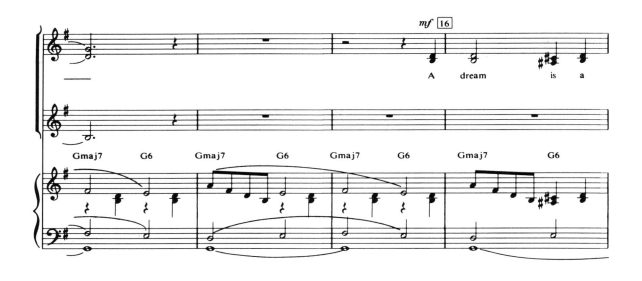

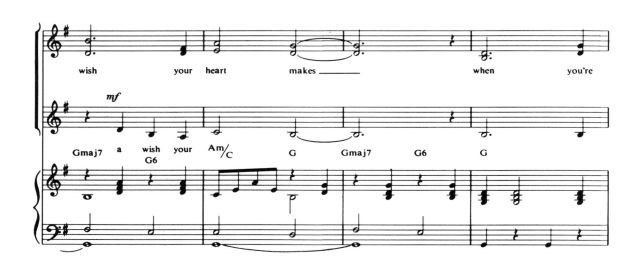

A Dream Is A Wish Your Heart Makes - SSA

A Dream Is A Wish Your Heart Makes - SSA

114

A Dream Is A Wish Your Heart Makes =SSA

A Dream Is A Wish Your Heart Makes - SSA

116

A Dream Is A Wish Your Heart Makes - SSA

Lo, How A Rose E'er Blooming

English version* by
Theodore Baker

Michael Praetorius (1572-1621)
Arranged by David Shand

The Lonely Goatherd

from "The Sound Of Music"

Arranged by Hale Smith

Lyrics by
OSCAR HAMMERSTEIN II

Music by
RICHARD RODGERS

quite re - mote, heard: lay - ee - o - dl, lay - ee - o - dl lay - ee - o.

quite re - mote, heard: lay - o - dl, lay - o - dl lay - ee - o.

quite re - mote, heard: lay - ee - o - dl lay - ee - o.

Lay - ee - o - dl, __ lay - ee - o - dl, lay - o - dl - lay - ee - o - dl - o.

Lay - ee - o - dl, __ lay - ee - o - dl, lay - ee - o - dl - lay - o - dl - o.

Lust - y and clear from the goat - herd's throat heard; lay - ee - o - dl - o.

122

124

Soon the du-et will be-come a tri-o, lay-ee o - dl, lay-ee o-dl-o.

Soon the du-et will be-come a tri-o, lay, lay o - dl - o.

Soon the du-et will be-come a tri-o, lay, lay o - dl - o.

Coda

Ho - di lay - ee _____ Ho - di lay - ee _____

Ho - di lay - ee __ Ho - di

Ho - di lay - ee __ Ho - di

to Gabriel Matoza

O Come, O Come, Emmanuel

From the ancient chant

RICHARD FELCIANO

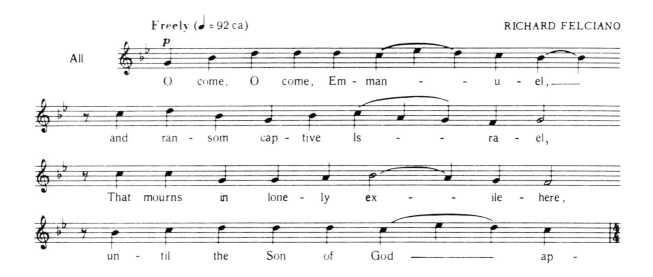

for Scott

One Small Child

By
JOYCE ELAINE EILERS

One wet kiss as he says "Good-night," One small child.

One wet kiss as he says "Good-night," One small child.

One wet kiss as he says "Good-night," One small child.

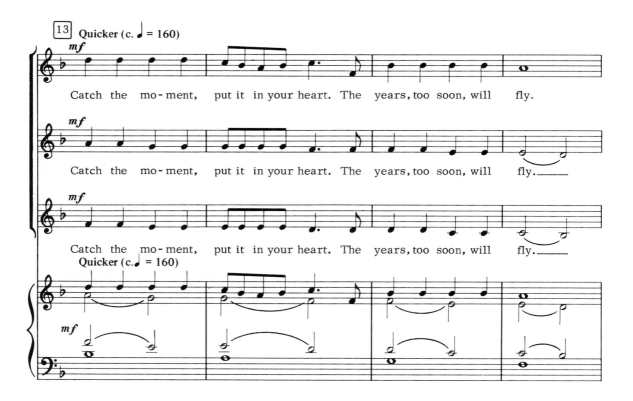

13 Quicker (c. ♩ = 160)

mf

Catch the mo-ment, put it in your heart. The years, too soon, will fly.

Catch the mo-ment, put it in your heart. The years, too soon, will fly.

Catch the mo-ment, put it in your heart. The years, too soon, will fly.

Quicker (c. ♩ = 160)

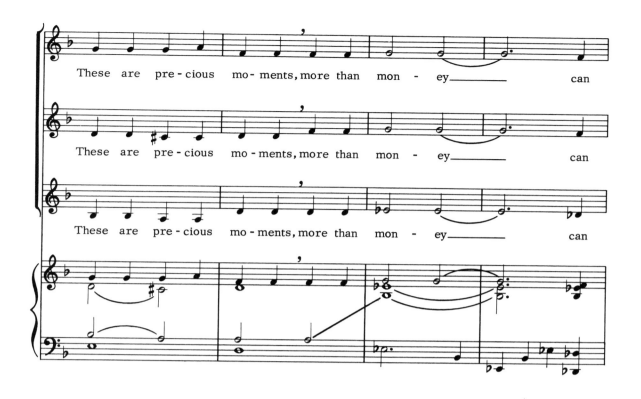

These are pre - cious mo - ments, more than mon - ey____ can

These are pre - cious mo - ments, more than mon - ey____ can

These are pre - cious mo - ments, more than mon - ey____ can

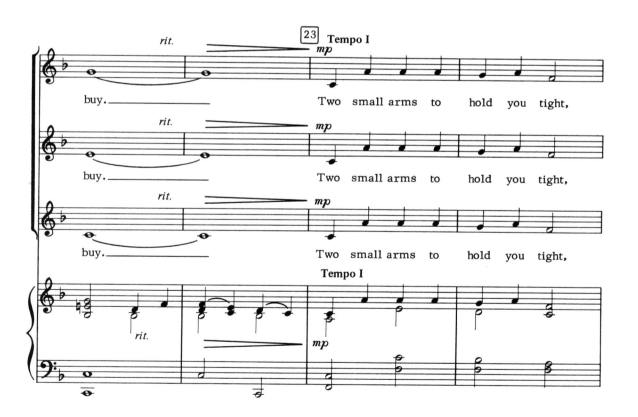

23 **Tempo I**

buy._____ Two small arms to hold you tight,

buy._____ Two small arms to hold you tight,

buy._____ Two small arms to hold you tight,

Tempo I

Two small feet to run, Two small eyes full of love for you,

Two small feet to run, Two small eyes full of love for you,

Two small feet to run, Two small eyes full of love for you,

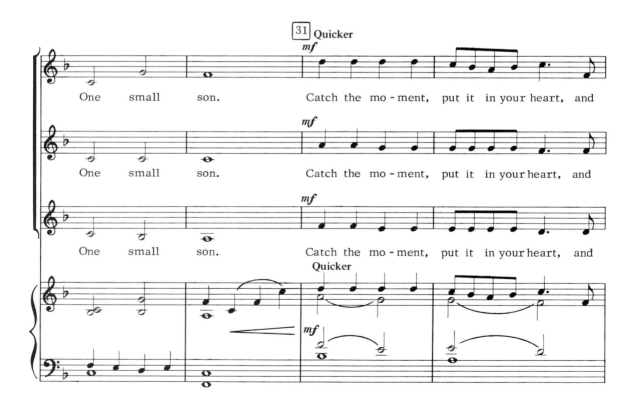

31 **Quicker**

One small son. Catch the mo - ment, put it in your heart, and

One small son. Catch the mo - ment, put it in your heart, and

One small son. Catch the mo - ment, put it in your heart, and

Quicker

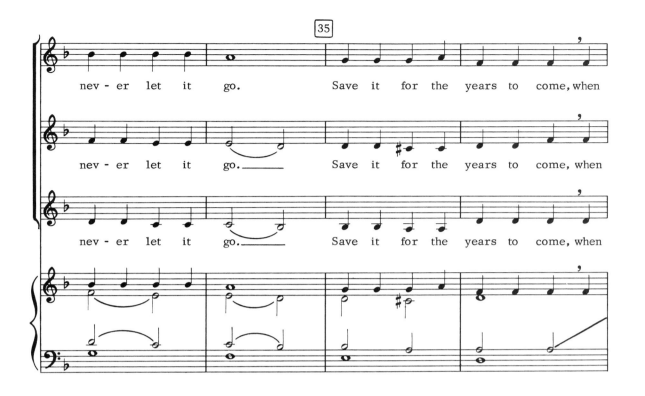

nev - er let it go. Save it for the years to come, when

nev - er let it go. Save it for the years to come, when

nev - er let it go. Save it for the years to come, when

41 Tempo I

he, too, will know One small hand to

he, too, will know One small hand to

he, too, will know One small hand to

a la music box

Pavane For Spring

ANONYMOUS

EUGENE BUTLER

Note: Recorders may double the voice parts.

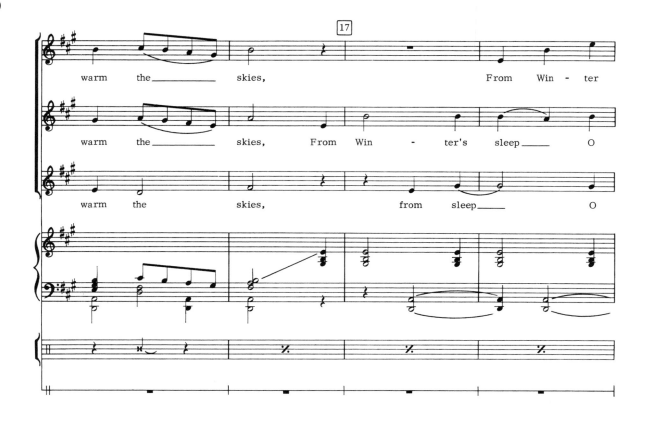

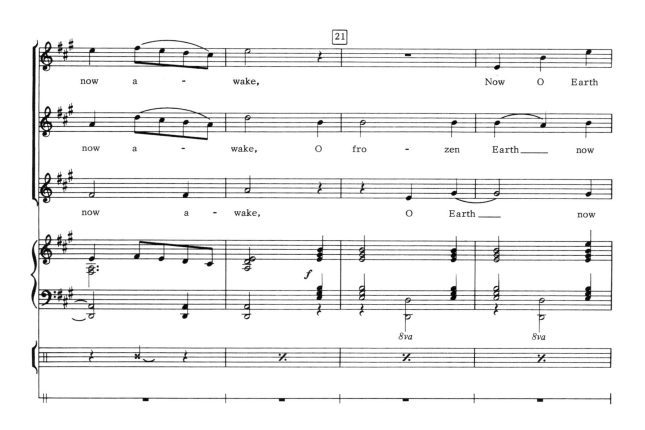

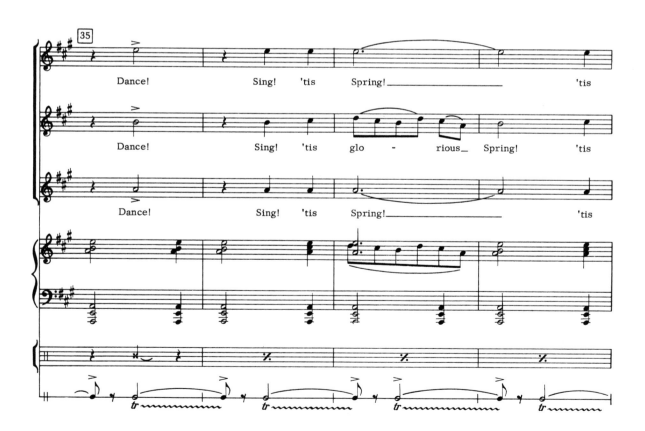

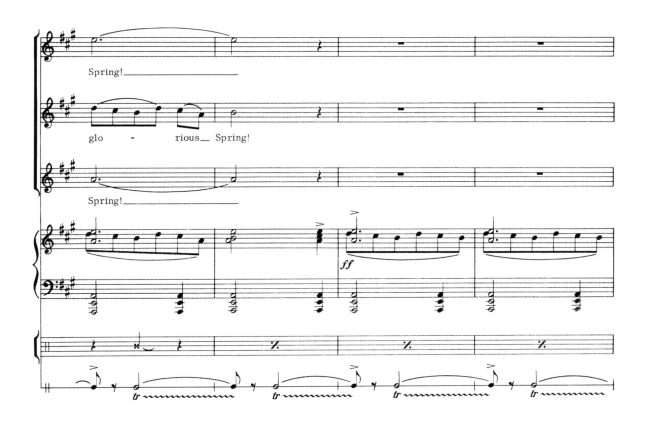

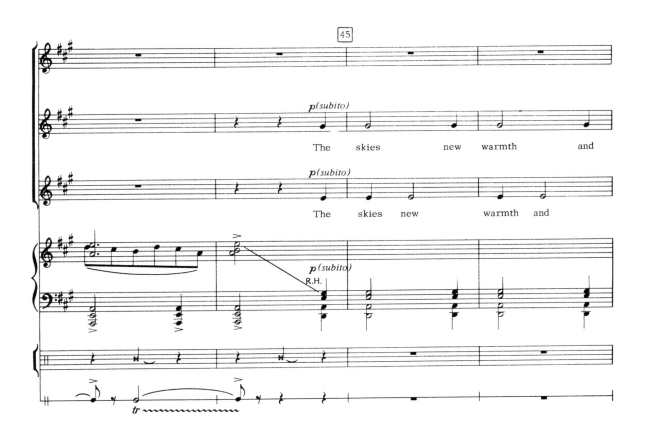

144

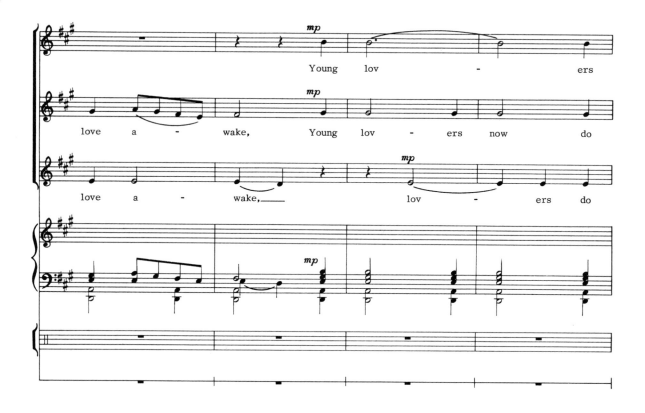

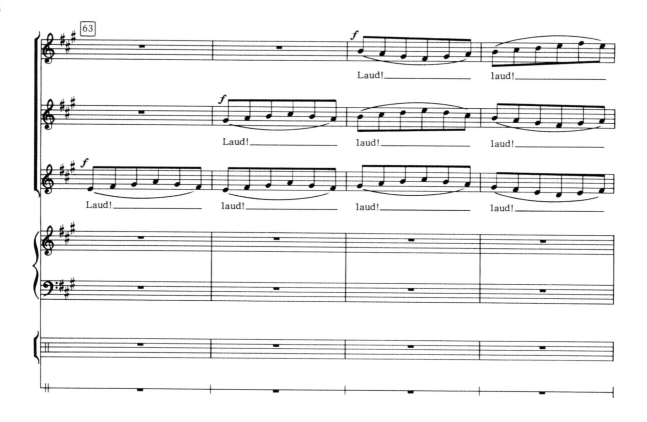

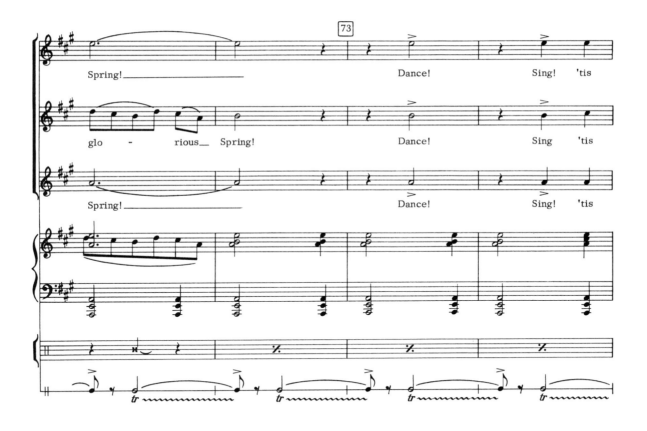

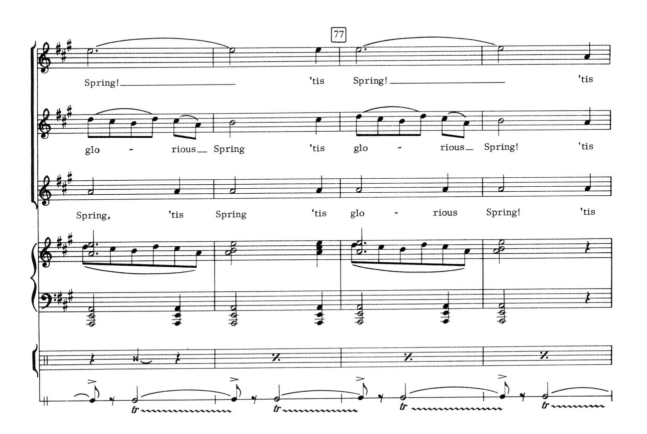

Shenandoah

American Folksong
Arranged by Margaret Vance

Shen - an - doah, _____ I long to hear you. _____

_____ A - way. _____

I'm bound _____ a - way, _____ 'Cross the

wide, _____ wide, _____ wide Mis - sou - ri. _____

152

Sing Aloud To God
(Effuderunt Sanguinem)

English text by R.G.P.

Michael Haydn
Edited by Reinhard G. Pauly

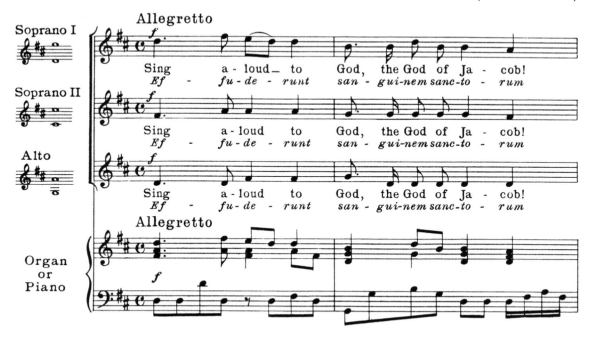

155

all the world shall pro-claim His great-ness, His great
qui ef-fu-sus, ef-fu-sus-est su - per

all the world shall pro-claim His great-ness, His great
qui ef-fu-sus, ef-fu-sus-est su - per

all the world shall pro-claim His great-ness, His great
qui ef-fu-sus, ef-fu-sus-est su - per

mer - cy. Sing a - loud to God, the God of Ja-cob!
ter - ram. Ef - fu - de - runt san-gui-nem sanc-to-rum,

mer - cy. Sing a - loud to God, the God of Ja-cob!
ter - ram. Ef - fu - de - runt san-gui-nem sanc-to-rum,

mer - cy. Sing a - loud to God, the God of Ja-cob!
ter - ram. Ef - fu - de - runt san-gui-nem sanc-to-rum,

Sing a - loud a joy - ful song to Him with harp and lyre, Je-ru - sa-
ef - fu - de - runt ve - lut a-quam in cir-cu - i - tu Je-ru - sa-

Sing a - loud a joy - ful song to Him with harp and lyre, Je ru - sa-
ef - fu - de - runt ve - lut a-quam in cir-cu - i - tu Je-ru - sa-

Sing a - loud a joy - ful song to Him with harp and lyre, Je ru - sa-
ef - fu - de - runt ve - lut a-quam in cir-cu - i - tu Je-ru - sa-

30 *p*

lem. He re-stor - eth the weak and need - y.
lem, et non e - rat, qui se-pe-li - ret.

lem. He re-stor - eth the weak and need - y.
lem, et non e - rat, qui se-pe-li - ret.

lem. He re-stor - eth the weak and need - y.
lem, et non e - rat, qui se-pe-li - ret.

mer - cy, His great mer - cy. Sing a - loud to God; Sing_
ter - ram, su - per ter - ram, qui ef - fu - sus est su -

mer - cy, His great mer - cy. Sing a - loud to God;
ter - ram, su - per ter - ram, qui ef - fu - sus est

mer - cy, His great mer - cy. Sing a - loud to God;
ter - ram, su - per ter - ram, qui ef - fu - sus est

_ a - loud to Him, sing a - loud to Him.
- per ter - ram, su-per ter - - ram.

Sing a - loud to Him, sing a - loud to Him.
su-per ter - ram, su-per ter - - ram.

Sing a - loud to Him, sing a - loud to Him.
su-per ter - ram, su-per ter - - ram.

Sunrise, Sunset
From the Musical "FIDDLER ON THE ROOF"

Words by SHELDON HARNICK
Music by JERRY BOCK
Arranged by RUTH ARTMAN

Performance Time: approx. 2:30

*Flute may be played an octave higher than written throughout. Other C instruments as notated.

Sun - rise,_____ Sun - set, Sun - rise,_____ Sun - set, Swift - ly_____

Sun - rise,_____ Sun - set, Sun - rise,_____ Sun - set, Swift - ly, _____

Sun - rise,_____ Sun - set, Sun - rise,_____ Sun - set, Swift - ly, _____

_____ fly the years;_____ One sea - son fol-low-ing an -

_____ swift - ly fly the years; One sea - son fol-low-ing an -

_____ swift - ly fly the years; One sea - son fol-low-ing an -

Ped._____ Ped._____

168

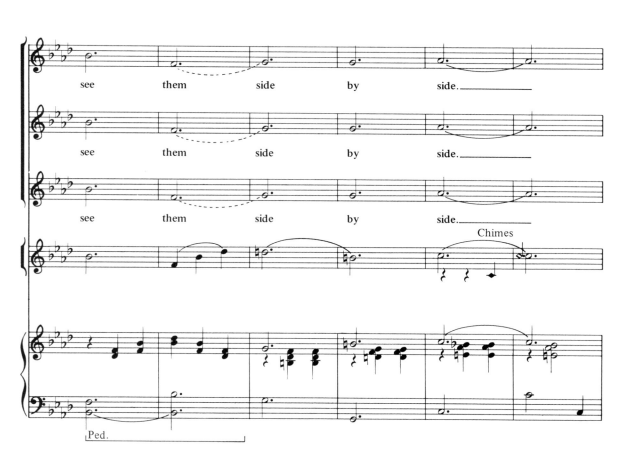

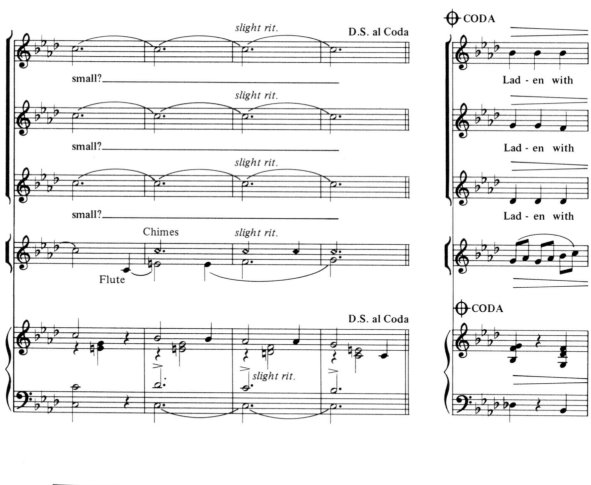

You Needed Me

Performance Notes:
Observe metronome marking carefully. Do not perform too fast. Keep all vocal and instrumental parts legato throughout. Vocalizing intervals of the octave, seventh and sixth in rehearsal will help the soprano section in singing this unusual but beautiful melody.
E.L.

Arranged by
ED LOJESKI

Performance time: approx. 3:38

Words and Music by
CHARLES RANDOLPH GOODRUM

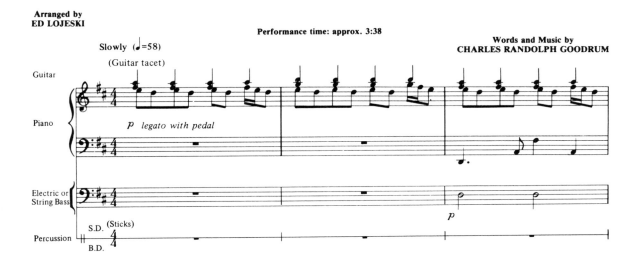

I cried a tear___ you wiped it dry, I was con-fused___

you cleared my mind. I sold my soul you bought it

Ah

Ah

cresc. *mp*

cresc. *mp*

back for me and held me up and gave me dig-ni-ty. Some-how you

Ah Some-how you

Ah Some-how you

lieve it's true,___ I need-ed you___ and you were there._____ And I'll

I need-ed you _____ and you were

I need-ed you _____ and you were

G   D/F#   Em7   G/D   D   F#7

nev - er leave_why should_I leave___ I'd be a fool,___ 'cause I've

there.   Oo

there.   Oo

Bm   D/A   G   D/F#

(Cym.)   (Closed Hi-Hat)

fin - 'lly found_ some-one who real - ly cares._

You held my hand_

some - one who

some-one who cares.

when it was cold, when I was lost_ you took me

cares. You held my hand when I was

You held my hand when it was cold, I was

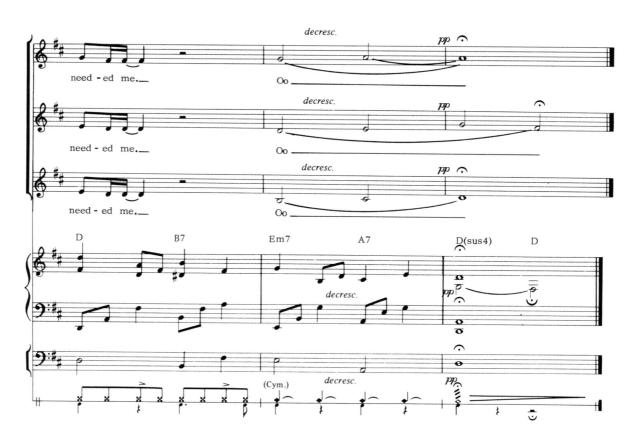

You Needed Me

Words and Music by
CHARLES RANDOLPH GOODRUM
·Arranged by ED LOJESKI

You Needed Me

Words and Music by
CHARLES RANDOLPH GOODRUM
Arranged by ED LOJESKI

You Needed Me

Words and Music by
CHARLES RANDOLPH GOODRUM
Arranged by ED LOJESKI

The Orchestra Song

English text by Marion Farquhar*

Traditional Austrian Song
Arranged by William Schuman

*Printed by exclusive permission

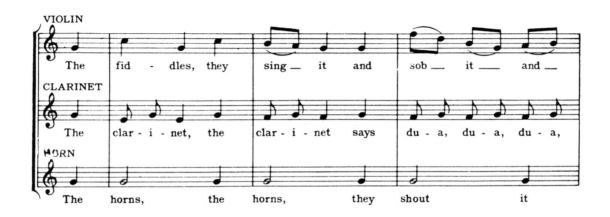

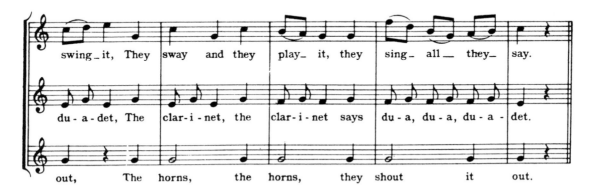

The drum has no troub-le, just doub-le dub doub-le, Five one, one five, *bum, bum, bum, bum, bum.

*Pronounce to rhyme with "drum".

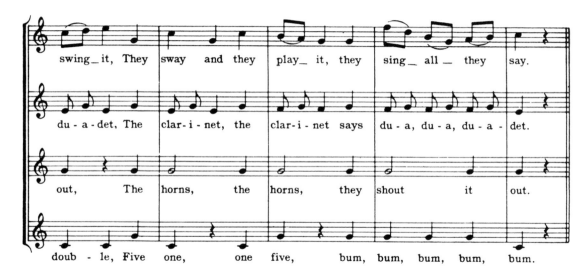

swing_ it, They sway and they play_ it, they sing _ all _ they say.

du - a - det, The clar - i - net, the clar-i-net says du - a, du - a, du - a - det.

out, The horns, the horns, they shout it out.

doub - le, Five one, one five, bum, bum, bum, bum, bum.

TRUMPET

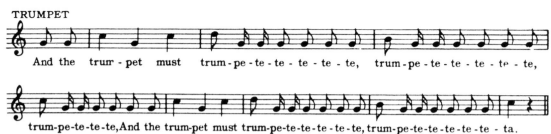

And the trum - pet must trum-pe-te-te-te-te, trum-pe-te-te-te-te,

trum-pe-te-te-te, And the trum-pet must trum-pe-te-te-te-te, trum-pe-te-te-te-te-ta.

VIOLIN

The fid - dles, they sing_ it and sob_ it _ and _

CLARINET

The clar - i - net, the clar - i - net says du - a, du - a, du - a,

HORN

The horns, the horns, they shout it

DRUM

The drum has no troub - le, just doub - le dub

TRUMPET

And the trum - pet must trum-pe-te-te-te-te, trum-pe-te - te - te - te,

185

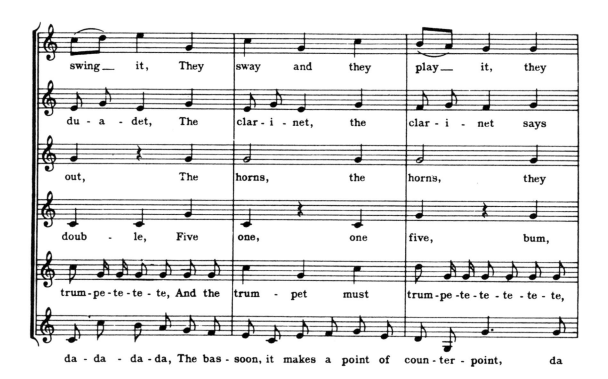

*An effective suggestion for performance is to sing these notes very long and loud, and suddenly start the last chorus *pp*

When Jesus Wept

From the New England
Psalm Singer, 1770

William Billings (1746–1800)
Edited by Don Gustafson

188

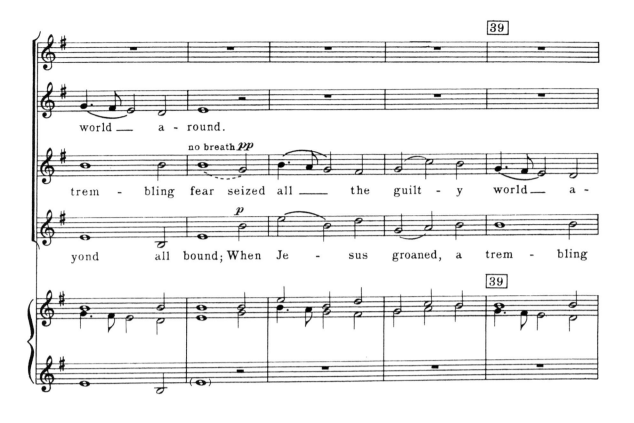

Alleluia

Duration: 1 min. 15 sec.

**English version by
Walter Ehret**

JOHANN SEBASTIAN BACH
Arranged by Walter Ehret

196

Boatmen Stomp (1979)

(from: the first set of New Songs to Old Words)

The Boatmen Dance by DD. Emmett

Michael A. Gray

O - hi - o!   Hi!   Ho!   the boat-men row!   Float-in' down the riv - er on the

O - hi - o!   Hi!   Ho!   the boat-men row!   Float-in' down the riv - er on the

O - hi - o!   Hi!   Ho!   the boat-men row!   Float-in' down the riv - er on the

O - hi - o!

O - hi - o!

O - hi - o!

sub. *p*

I Wonder As I Wander

Collected by
John Jacob Niles

Appalachian Carol
Adapted and arranged by
John Jacob Niles and Lewis Henry Horton

Lovers Love The Spring

Duration: 1 min., 5 sec.
from Shakespeare's
"As You Like It"

ARTHUR FRACKENPOHL

1 Also published for SSA and SATB, both with Piano.
2 String bass to play pizz with Piano l.h. throughout--upper notes or cue size notes when present.
3 ♩. ♪ = ♪ ♪ ♪ throughout

210

Piping Tim Of Galway
(from: Sing Out Young Voices, Vol. 1)

Frederick Swanson

216

count-ing_ sleep a thing to scorn.__ Old is__ he, but not out-worn,

count-ing_ sleep a thing to scorn. Old is__ he, but not out-worn,

D. S. al ⊕

Pip - ing Tim of Gal - way.

Pip - ing_ Tim of Gal - way.

D. S. al ⊕

⊕ *Coda*

Pip - ing_ Tim, Pip - ing_ Tim of Gal - way.

Pip - ing_ Tim, Pip - ing_ Tim of Gal - way.

⊕ *Coda*

Rudolph The Red-Nosed Reindeer

Performance Notes:

Observe all tempo and rhythmic markings carefully. Note that at Letter B all eighth notes should be played exactly as written without any swing or jazz feeling whatsoever. The swing rhythm feeling does not occur until two measures prior to Letter D. Keep accompaniment understated throughout and rather on the light side.

Arranged by
ED LOJESKI

E.L.

Performance time: approx. 2:45

Words and Music by
JOHNNY MARKS

*Available for:
SATB, SAB, SSA, TBB, Two Part

RUDOLPH THE RED-NOSED REINDEER - TBB

220

RUDOLPH THE RED-NOSED REINDEER - TBB

Then how the rein - deer loved him_ as they shout-ed out with glee: _____

Then how the rein - deer loved him_ as they shout-ed out with glee: _____

Then how the rein - deer loved him_ as they shout-ed out with glee: _____

"Ru - dolph, red - nosed rein - deer,_ you'll go down in his - to - ry!"_____

"Ru-dolph, the red - nosed rein - deer,_ you'll go down in his - to - ry!"_____

"Ru-dolph, the red - nosed rein - deer,_ you'll go down in his - to - ry!"_____

(Bells)

RUDOLPH THE RED-NOSED REINDEER - TBB

RUDOLPH THE RED-NOSED REINDEER - TBB

224

RUDOLPH THE RED-NOSED REINDEER - TBB